CAPITOL REEF
CANYON COUNTRY EDEN

CAPITOL REEF
CANYON COUNTRY EDEN

Rose Houk

Capitol Reef Natural History Association
Torrey, Utah

First Printing

Author: Rose Houk
Editor: John Evarts
Graphic designer: Katey O'Neill
Photo captions: John Evarts
Printed in the United States at Lorraine Press, Salt Lake City

Produced by:
Cachuma Press
P.O. Box 560
Los Olivos, California 93441

To order this book, please contact the publisher at:
Capitol Reef Natural History Association
Capitol Reef National Park
HC 70 Box 15
Torrey, Utah 84775-9602

Library of Congress Catalog Card Number: 95-83492
ISBN (paperback): 1-887517-00-6   ISBN (cloth): 1-887517-01-4

ACKNOWLEDGMENTS

The author is grateful for the assistance of several people in writing the text for this book. Robert Mack and Rick Nolan of Capitol Reef National Park assisted throughout the project. Jim Mead and John MacDonald kindly shared their scientific knowledge, and orchard keeper Kent Jackson related the fascinating history of Fruita's orchards. John Evarts of Cachuma Press and Shirley Torgerson of the Capitol Reef Natural History Association were instrumental in this book becoming reality. And as always, thanks to my husband, Michael Collier, who first showed me this wonderful place called Capitol Reef.

Front cover: © GEORGE H. H. HUEY *(background) and* © LARRY ULRICH *(inset)*
Back cover: © CARR CLIFTON
Half-title page: © DAVID EDE
Title-page spread: © JOHN TELFORD
Contents page: © STEPHEN TRIMBLE

CONTENTS

FOREWORD

The Southwest's high-desert province known as the Colorado Plateau encompasses more magnificent scenery than any comparable-sized area of North America. Monument Valley, the Grand Canyon, Zion, Bryce, Arches, Canyonlands, and Mesa Verde are just a few of the world-renowned treasures that belong to this celebrated landscape. In a region endowed with such an abundance of natural beauty, it is perhaps no surprise that, until recent years, Capitol Reef National Park was overshadowed by some of its more famous neighbors. Yet Capitol Reef has always claimed legions of admirers, many of whom still fondly recall the years prior to 1962, when the Park's primary access was an unpaved route through the flash flood-prone narrows of Capitol Gorge.

After Capitol Reef was established as a National Monument in 1937, one of its frequent visitors was author and wilderness advocate Wallace Stegner. In his seminal work, *Mormon Country* (1942), Stegner described the scene:

> "The country is spectacular and almost inaccessible . . . . The terrain is so broken and eroded that even yet parts of the monument have not been explored, and in 1940 a party discovered a natural bridge that had remained hidden for sixty-five years, though it was only three miles from the town of Fruita. In country like that, habits linger."

More than half a century later, Stegner's assessment still rings true. Capitol Reef and its historic focal point, Fruita, remain largely unblemished by overcrowding, traffic jams, creeping urbanization, or other maladies that often afflict more popular parks and monuments.

The Waterpocket Fold's magnificent western escarpment looms above Park headquarters and beckons visitors to get acquainted with Capitol Reef's remarkable geologic story. © JEFF NICHOLAS.
Opposite: Like other streams that flow through the Waterpocket Fold, Sulphur Creek has helped shape the rich natural and cultural history of Capitol Reef. © STEPHEN TRIMBLE.

Beyond the chiseled cliffs that tower over Fruita's bucolic orchards lie thousands of acres of remote, arid, and exquisitely sculpted wilderness. A handful of rutted dirt roads thread through the Park's spectacular backcountry, traversing some of southern Utah's loneliest mesas, canyons, and badlands. Capitol Reef's principal neighbors are ranchers and farmers whose lifestyles are not vastly different from the pioneers who first settled the territory.

For this book, author Rose Houk has written six poignant essays that express a deep, but unpretentious appreciation of Capitol Reef. She is intimately acquainted with this inspiring and uncompromising land. During many years as a resident of the Colorado Plateau, Rose has returned to the Park time and again, exploring slickrock canyons, marveling at the epic geology of the Waterpocket Fold, and studying the Fremont people whose culture was centered here. For her, Capitol Reef is "a place of reverence and joy." The accompanying images represent the work of landscape photographers from Utah and throughout the West. Their evocative photographs offer us more than a gallery of pretty pictures; they reveal the unique character and unexpected diversity of Capitol Reef.

This book pays tribute to a very special place. Its publisher, the Capitol Reef Natural History Association, has many members who are lifelong neighbors of the Park. It is their hope, shared by all who have participated in this project, that this publication will engender a broader understanding of Capitol Reef and strengthen our resolve to be responsible stewards of Utah's canyon country Eden.

—John Evarts

LAY OF THE LAND

My introduction to Capitol Reef came in wintertime many years ago. During that first unforgettable encounter, my husband and I spent several days on the east side of the Waterpocket Fold. We hiked up canyon after canyon, venturing into places with names like Burro Wash, Oak Creek, and Pleasant Creek. Whenever a canyon ended in some unscalable spot, we backtracked and climbed up onto the slickrock sandstone and surveyed our surroundings.

To the east, the gray pleats of the Mancos Cliffs skirted the front of the crisp, snow-capped peaks of the Henry Mountains. Off to the south were the Circle Cliffs and the unseen turquoise waters of Lake Powell. To the west loomed the big blue hump of Boulder Mountain. To the north, the long backbone of the Waterpocket Fold stretched as far as we could see.

During that trip I began to feel the lay of the land and learn some of its hidden secrets. I followed streambeds that twisted and turned until they nearly doubled back on themselves, explored alcoves in sheer sandstone cliffs, examined ripple-marked boulders, and watched clouds reflected in a small pocket of water held within the rock. Capitol Reef was working its magic on me.

The landscapes we know and return to become places of solace. We are drawn to them because of the stories they tell, because of the memories they hold, or simply because of the sheer beauty that calls us back again and again.

—Terry Tempest Williams
The Canyon's Edge, 1986

Sunset light glows from cliffs, crags, and domes along the western wall of the Waterpocket Fold (above). © ROD PLANCK.
Preceding pages: Sulphur Creek cuts a deep, winding canyon on its path through the Fold's many layers (left). © TOM TILL.
A father and daughter wade upstream in the Fremont River near Fruita (right). © STEPHEN TRIMBLE.

The 241,671 acres of Capitol Reef National Park lie in a long, narrow north-south corridor that closely parallels the natural boundaries of the Waterpocket Fold. The Fold is a raised and dramatically tilted swell of rock that stretches sinuously through southern Utah for a hundred miles. Capitol Reef takes its name from prominent features of the Fold. A rounded dome of golden-white sandstone that caps the Fold is suggestive of the rotunda of the United States Capitol building and is the source of the first part of the name. The second part was inspired by the Waterpocket Fold: pioneers found it a barrier to travel, reminding them of barrier reefs in the ocean.

When geologist Grove Karl Gilbert passed through Capitol Reef in 1875, he observed that this deeply carved land is "a dissection which lays bare the very anatomy of the rocks." That anatomy exposes, in spectacular glory, a quarter billion years of earth's history, from the time when this area was a coastal region through the age of the dinosaurs. Though these rocks appear static, water and wind are still very much at work, shaping the colorful domes, knobs, and canyons that contribute to the captivating scenery of Capitol Reef.

In addition to its wonderland of rocks, the high-desert landscape of Capitol Reef is blessed by the presence of water. The Fremont River, the Park's paramount stream, makes a dramatic passage through the Waterpocket Fold. The river was named for western explorer John Charles Frémont, who saw the stream in the winter of 1853–54 while camped about twenty-five miles northwest of Capitol Reef near the present-day town of Fremont.

The Fremont River has served as a corridor for human passage for millennia. A distinct culture, known as the Fremont, lived along its banks in Capitol Reef from about 700 to 1300 A.D. In more recent times, bands of Paiutes and Utes camped and wintered along the Fremont and its tributaries; unlike their predecessors, they left few traces of their presence. In the late-nineteenth century, hardy Mormon farm families settled on the flood plain of the Fremont and founded a community that eventually became known as Fruita.

The rich tapestry of human history in Capitol Reef is interwoven with a diverse natural history. Habitats range from low, warm desert in the far south end of the Park where delicate

Western bristlecone pines grow in a remote, high-elevation site in Capitol Reef. Gnarled and picturesque even after death, these trees are one of earth's most long-lived organisms. © DAVID EDE.

The white evening primrose, which opens its petals late in the day, is a delicate and sweet-scented wildflower that graces many Capitol Reef trails (above). © ROD PLANCK.

A hiker approaches the summit of Fern's Nipple, one of the Park's most distinctive Navajo Sandstone domes (above, right). © DAVID PLATT.

wildflowers grow amid barren sand and rock, to high, cool uplands where ancient bristlecone pines survive on forested plateaus. Throughout this arid country, water makes its presence known in surprising ways. Dry streams suddenly flow during summer thunderstorms, fern gardens festoon moist clefts in sandstone walls, and waterpockets brim with seasonal runoff.

I never suspected on my first trip here that I'd be back as many times as I have, seeking the clear desert air, wild beauty, peaceful solitude, and human stories of Capitol Reef. It has become one of my favorite places in the universe, a place where I come for my sanity, my serenity, and my soul. It is for me a place of exploration and inspiration, a place of reverence and joy.

Naturally eroded rock basins, called waterpockets, are found throughout the Fold, especially on sandstone ledges, benches, and other exposed outcrops. They capture and hold ephemeral runoff, providing a critical source of water to wildlife and backcountry hikers.

© MARC MUENCH.

*E*nthralling vistas, such as this
overlook at Upper Cathedral Valley,
greet visitors who venture into the
Park's remote northern sections.
© CARR CLIFTON.

*Opposite: Capitol Reef's golden
sandstone summits become luminous
at dusk.* © LARRY ULRICH.

*Preceding pages: This panoramic
view reveals the sedimentary "layer-
cake" that has been uplifted along
the western face of the Waterpocket
Fold.* © GEORGE H. H. HUEY.

junction of the Fremont River and Sulphur Creek. They correctly surmised that this location's alluvial soils, lower elevation, and ready supply of irrigation water made an ideal spot for raising fruit and other crops.

Nels Johnson claimed the first permanent homestead here in 1880 and others soon followed. The new townsite was known as Junction, a name retained until 1904 when it was changed to Fruita. Nels and his neighbors watched for the first pinkish-white blossoms to open on the apricot trees, knowing that spring snowmelt would soon swell the river and provide ample water for their irrigation ditches. Fremont River water was channeled to orchards, hayfields, and row crops as farmers transformed the canyon bottom into a verdant oasis. As early as 1898, Rabbit Valley resident Franklin W. Young called Fruita the "Eden of Wayne County."

Fruita remained a small outpost on the Mormon frontier, never growing much in population. Only about ten families lived in the community, and everyone knew everyone else. Along with Nels Johnson and his brother John, the Jorgensons, Behunins, Pierces, Mulfords, Cooks, Clarkes, Oylers, Chesnuts, and Holts were among the first to build homes, plant trees, and beget children.

As I spend time in Fruita, I wonder what life was like for Rena Holt. She and her husband Leo were among Fruita's earliest settlers, living in a boarded tent when they first arrived. Certainly Rena knew well the joys and heartaches of bearing children in a place so far from medical help. As the local midwife, she helped usher more than fifty babies into the world. I suspect on more than one occasion

The Fremont River flows east through the Park (above).
© MARK J. DOLYAK.
Many apple varieties grow in Fruita (opposite, above).
© CARA MOORE.
A chukar struts near Fruita's campground (opposite, below).
© ROD PLANCK.
Preceding pages: Historic barn in Fruita (left). © SCOTT T. SMITH.
Fruita's schoolhouse was completed at the base of redrock cliffs in 1896 (right). © MARK J. DOLYAK.

Rena was roused out in the middle of the night by a frantic husband whose wife was in labor. Hitching the wagon, she'd head off into the darkness, doing the best she could with what was available. She also knew great sorrow when her first child, a girl, died at three months of age from a scorpion sting.

Leo Holt was a carpenter and stonemason, and he helped build Fruita's one-room schoolhouse in 1892. The school remained in use until 1941, when the students were sent to a larger, more centrally located school in a nearby town. The schoolhouse served both social and religious functions too, for this Mormon village

never got its own bishop or official church building.

Rena, Leo, and all their neighbors knew the meaning of hard work. They spent much of the summer and early fall picking, packing, and canning fruit. A choice jar of perfect peaches uncapped for a special winter supper stirred memories of wonderful summer days. There were always trees to prune, cows to milk, bread to bake, quilts to stitch, and, once in a while, the diversion of a picnic, dance, or sandlot baseball game.

Produce and its byproducts were Fruita's claim to fame. Fruit and vegetables, along with wine and moonshine, were almost always available for sale or barter. Passing stockmen could rely on finding something to settle the dust in their throats at the camp house, built near what is now the Pendleton-Jorgenson-Gifford barn.

Aside from the occasional passerby, contact with the outside world was infrequent. Before Fruita got a post office in 1904, mail was delivered by horseback or wagon and placed into boxes nailed to a cottonwood tree near the center of town. On mail day, everyone congregated around the "mail tree," anxious for welcome words from distant friends and family. The mail tree and another huge cottonwood beside it, each about a century old, still stand in the picnic area.

Fruita's isolation was ensured by bad roads. The first wagon road into the canyon required many river crossings; residents soon carved an alternative route through Capitol Gorge, a few miles south of Fruita. This road was a bit of an improvement, but it was often subject to flash floods.

Capitol Gorge is now open only to hikers, many of whom come to see the Pioneer Register where nineteenth- and early twentieth-century travelers etched their names into the cliff wall. The earliest names inscribed in the rock belong to J.A. Call and Walt Bateman, who passed through on September 20, 1871. As I walk this historic route, I am astounded by the fact that this road, no wider than a wagon in places, offered the only way through the Waterpocket Fold until 1962, when State Highway 24 was built.

After the turn of the century, Fruita became a better-known destination for people from the "outside." Resident Clarence Mulford guided archaeologist Noel Morss around Capitol Reef in the summers of 1928 and 1929. Morss was investigating the

*E*arly-day travelers through Capitol Gorge often inscribed their names on the narrow canyon walls. © LYNN RADEKA.
Fruita's settlers took advantage of the mild microclimate along the lower Fremont River to grow a wide variety of fruit, including apricots (opposite). © LARRY VENSEL.

prehistory of the area for Harvard's Peabody Museum. He expected to find remains like those of the Anasazi, who had lived to the south, but what Morss encountered was different.

Near Fruita, the archaeologist discovered distinctive buckskin moccasins made from the hides of mountain sheep; some of the moccasins still had dewclaws attached to the soles. He collected clay figurines, mats of twined juniper bark, pieces of pottery and fur blankets, corncobs, planting sticks, and grinding stones. Morss also found small structures beneath ledges. Built from sandstone slabs and supported by wooden poles, these shelters were perhaps the temporary homes of Fruita's prehistoric people. He observed fantastic drawings that had been pecked and painted into cliffs overlooking the Fremont River: animated likenesses of bighorn sheep and unusual humanlike figures portrayed with elaborate headdresses and jewelry. From what he saw and recorded along the Fremont River near Fruita, Morss defined a culture that he called the Fremont, people who preceded the Mormon pioneers by almost a thousand years.

Within a few years of Morss's visit, the wonders of Capitol Reef came to the attention of the federal government. In 1932, agent Roger Toll was sent to determine the worthiness of Capitol Reef as a national monument. During his visit, Toll reported that Fruita was then "two ranches and a roadside store." On the 1932 road map, there was not a paved road in this portion of Utah.

Capitol Reef was designated as a national monument in 1937. The first superintendent, Charles Kelly, took up residence in the

house that had once belonged to Rena and Leo Holt. A prolific author and colorful character, Kelly was also an outspoken advocate for the Park. When uranium prospectors swarmed over the area in the 1950s, he expressed strong opposition to mineral exploration within the monument. In 1971, Capitol Reef became a national park.

Today, Capitol Reef attracts hundreds of thousands of people each year, the majority of whom come to Fruita. Like many of them, I pay a visit to the old schoolhouse. Sitting quietly outside, I imagine I hear the words of a hymn pouring out of the windows into the green orchard, words that flowed so gladly from the hearts of Rena Holt and the other Fruita pioneers:

> Lo! in the desert the flowers are springing;
> Streams, ever copious, are gliding along.
> Loud from the mountaintops echoes are ringing;
> Wastes rise in verdure and mingle in song.

*F*ruita's orchards are reminders of the agrarian community that once flourished here. © SCOTT T. SMITH.

Opposite page, clockwise from upper left: One of the area's first pioneers, Elijah Cutler Behunin, built this cabin a few miles downriver from Fruita in 1882. © SCOTT T. SMITH.

Relics typical of Fruita's past are found in the Park's historic district. © DAVID EDE.

A wood-burning stove heated the Fruita schoolhouse. © JUDIE CHROBAK-COX.

Wheelwrights demonstrate their craft during a fall harvest celebration. © STEPHEN TRIMBLE.

West of Fruita, fluted walls of soft Moenkopi sediments culminate in the 660-foot-high landmark known as Chimney Rock. A cap of the harder Shinarump rock protects this column and the adjacent cliffs from more rapid erosion. © LARRY ULRICH. *Opposite: Rising east of Park headquarters is a magnificent butte known as the Castle; its distinct layers of red Moenkopi and gray-green Chinle are topped by chiseled ramparts of Wingate Sandstone.* © DAVID MUENCH.

Capitol Dome overlooks the gorge of the Fremont River; its rounded summit is about 630 feet above the canyon floor. © WILLIAM M. SMITHEY, JR.

Opposite: Upper South Desert Overlook offers a classic Colorado Plateau vista: a wondrous expanse of deeply eroded mesas, basins, buttes, and canyons, framed by the distant heights of snow-covered peaks. The Henry Mountains, capped by 11,522-foot-high Mt. Ellen, lie about forty miles southeast of Fruita. © JEFF GNASS.

*T*he graceful profile of Brimhall
Double Bridge soars above a narrow
side canyon of Halls Creek. The
bridge is named in honor of the late
Dean Brimhall of Fruita, an expert
on southern Utah's Native American
rock art. © TOM TILL.

*Opposite: Clouds and storms often
create dramatic lighting at Capitol
Reef and intensify the stark beauty of
the land.* © WILLIAM M. SMITHEY, JR.

A History in Stone

My walk up Sheets Gulch begins near the Notom Road and, as usual, the plants attract my attention. On this fine September morning a variety of wildflowers is still in bloom. A scarlet gilia blazes in solitary beauty in the bed of the wash. Dainty starlike flowers wave atop slender wire lettuce that spills from the cliffs. An outstanding yellow beeplant swarms with tiny pollinators. Masses of flowers on longleaf brickellbush perfume the air with each down-canyon breeze.

But what really stands out here—as elsewhere in this national park—are the rocks. They are the heart and soul of Capitol Reef. Sheets Gulch cuts through the Park's most renowned geologic feature, the Waterpocket Fold. The Fold is a multi-layered flexure of rock that rises 2,000 feet and extends a hundred miles, from Thousand Lake Mountain to the Colorado River.

The fantastic rocky wonderland of Capitol Reef and the Waterpocket Fold is built primarily of sediments—lots of sediments delivered by air and water. Between 100 and 200 million years ago, rivers and seas and winds stacked up nearly ten thousand feet of silts, clays, and sands. These materials were gradually cemented into the

> *There is an enchantment in these dry canyons that once roared with water and still sometimes do . . . something of massive dignity about sandstone beds that tell of a past long before human breathing, that bear the patterns of ancient winds and water in their crossbeddings.*
>
> **—Ann Zwinger**
> ***Wind in the Rock, 1978***

bold and colorful siltstones, mudstones, and sandstones we see in Capitol Reef today.

About sixty-five million years ago, when these layers of rock were still at or below sea level, powerful tectonic movements squeezed them in an east-west direction. The rocks were bent into a half arch, or monocline as geologists call it. Approximately seventeen million years ago, the 130,000-square-mile Colorado Plateau, including Capitol Reef, was uplifted about twelve thousand feet above sea level. Over time, erosion stripped away the exposed, softer sediments, like a curtain pulled back to reveal a stage. The rock layers that had been buckled earlier were now in full view.

To get your geological bearings in the Fold, it helps to use your imagination. First envision thousands of feet of rock once here, laid up in a neat, unbent stack. Next imagine the layers being squeezed together and forming something like a rounded stairstep. Then view the upraised Fold; its upper layers have been worn away and the now-visible underlying layers tilt skyward in herringbone chevrons of salmon, ivory, and lavender.

Not only has erosion unveiled the monocline, it has also etched the countless canyons that crease the Fold, including Sheets Gulch. Water cuts down from the Fold's higher western side to its lower eastern side; with each downpour and flash flood, it further scours and deepens these desert canyons. Although Sheets Gulch is dry on this day, I see ample evidence of water's passage: polygon mosaics of cracked mud; pebbles and rocks facing downstream like neatly layered tiles; clots of sticks, pine needles, and cottonwood

*F*lash floods have polished the walls of this slot canyon in the Fold (above). © GEORGE H. H. HUEY. *Preceding pages: This aerial view of the southern Waterpocket Fold shows the uptilted and eroded formations along the eastern side of the monocline (left).* © WM. B. DEWEY. *Layers of deposition are visible in this sandstone (right).* © LEO LARSON.

leaves; and a huge log of pine or fir, rafted down from the high country during a big flood.

I follow Sheets Gulch west, and as I go deeper into the Fold the uptilted formations I pass become successively older. For about a half mile the canyon remains relatively open, but then the walls suddenly close in. I have entered the domain of Navajo Sandstone, the rock that forms the backbone of Capitol Reef. The Navajo is made of tiny grains of nearly pure quartz that once existed as dunes in a deep sand "sea" covering southeast Utah and northeast Arizona. Then one of the world's largest sand deposits, it has since turned to stone. Surrounded by this rock, I feel like I have gone inside the earth.

The tawny Navajo Sandstone is swirled and honeycombed, swept into elegant crossbeds that trace the path of ancient winds. Frosty grain by frosty grain, it erodes to form knobby domes and

Sheets Gulch opens a deep, narrow cleft through Navajo, Kayenta, and Wingate sandstones, and allows hikers to make a scenic passage through the Fold (above, left).
© LARRY VENSEL.

The walls of Sheets Gulch have been scoured smooth by silt-laden waters (above). © STEVE MULLIGAN.

With their diverse textures, colors, and shapes, the rocks of Capitol Reef are captivating for their beauty as well as their geology. © PHILIP HYDE.
Opposite page, clockwise from upper left: Desert varnish has left a rich patina on this arch. © GEORGE H. H. HUEY. *Weathering has honeycombed this alcove.* © WILLIAM NEILL.
Lichens encrust one side of this fractured panel. © ROD PLANCK. *A tiny stream of sand grains threads a path between canyon walls.* © LARRY ULRICH.

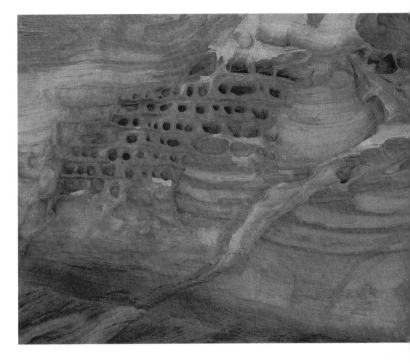

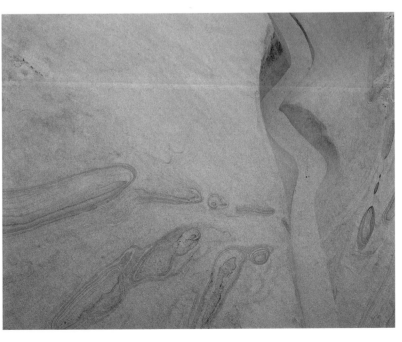

*S*panish bayonet yucca blooms atop the Waterpocket Fold.

© FRED HIRSCHMANN.

Opposite: Strike Valley Overlook provides an ideal perspective for gaining an appreciation of the Waterpocket Fold. The Fold's formations were laid down about 100 to 200 million years ago, mostly forming as deposits in shallow seas or swamps, or as sand dunes. These layers flexed upward here 60 to 70 million years ago. Subsequent uplift and erosion completed the sculpting of this geologic spectacle.

© FRED HIRSCHMANN.

The stone temples of Capitol Reef may appear immutable, but even the hardest rock eventually breaks down into tiny grains. Sulphur Creek's silty water is a reminder of this inexorable process. © SCOTT T. SMITH. *Opposite: Sculpted in Kayenta Sandstone, Hickman Bridge is one of the premier natural landmarks in Capitol Reef. Its name commemorates Joseph S. Hickman, a local educator and legislator whose efforts helped lead to the establishment of Capitol Reef National Monument in 1937.* © DAVID MUENCH.

Rising some 400 feet from the floor of Lower Cathedral Valley, the Temple of the Sun is an awe-inspiring sight, especially when its salmon-pink ramparts become radiant in the light of dawn. Sandstone monoliths like this are found nowhere else on the Colorado Plateau. © JACK DYKINGA.

*L*andscape photographers often shoot during the dawn or dusk, seeking images that record "the edge of light." These Navajo Sandstone domes, with oval caps of the Carmel Formation, are bathed in the soft, warm light of sunset. © WILLIAM M. SMITHEY, JR.

ENCHANTED SURPRISE

Every hike, I believe, is blessed with at least one welcome surprise. As I prepare to walk down Pleasant Creek, I subconsciously wait for what this day will bring.

My trail begins near an old corral, about all that remains of the homestead of Ephraim and Thisbe Hanks. These Latter-day Saints settled in this wild spot in 1881 and called it Floral Ranch, renamed Sleeping Rainbow Ranch by later owners. It was here that "Brother Eph" Hanks grew good crops of sugar cane, perhaps for use in the distillery he allegedly maintained. Floral Ranch was also raided by federal marshals, who often came in search of fugitive polygamists who they suspected the Hanks were harboring.

Even before Eph and his young wife arrived at Pleasant Creek, Hanks had led a remarkable life. He sailed the high seas, carried U.S. mail across the mountains on snowshoe, and brought food to a beleaguered Mormon handcart company during their 1,400-mile walk to Salt Lake City in 1856. When Hanks died in 1896, his daughter-in-law declared in his obituary that God gave him "the power to raise the dead, heal the sick, and cure frozen limbs." Indeed, his seventy years were filled with more living than most of us

It is a maze of cliffs and terraces lined off with stratification, of crumbling buttes, red and white domes, rock platforms gashed with profound canyons, burning plains . . . . It is the extreme of desolation, the blankest solitude, a superlative desert.
—**Clarence Dutton**
Report on the Geology of the High Plateaus of Utah, 1880

Pleasant Creek flows across a bedrock of Navajo Sandstone (above). © D. A. HORCHNER.
Boulder Mountain vista near Pleasant Creek's headwaters (opposite, above). © CARA MOORE.
Cottonwood leaves decorate a moist sandbar (opposite, below). © LEO LARSON.
Preceding pages: Pleasant Creek gently meanders east of the Fold (left). © SCOTT T. SMITH.
Capitol Reef's rugged topography discouraged nineteenth-century explorers (right). © LARRY VENSEL.

could ever imagine.

I ponder pioneers of such resolve and fiber as I follow Pleasant Creek on this warm July day. Soon I hear the magical sound of flowing water, even before I see it. Like many people before me, I am drawn to Pleasant Creek by its most precious gift: water in an arid country. The stream's clear, warm current flows through the very heart of the Waterpocket Fold. Lined with cottonwoods, willows, and sedges, Pleasant Creek empties into the Fremont River, and along with the Fremont, it is one of the few year-round watercourses in Capitol Reef.

As I trod over soft sand, past prickly pear and black boulders, I imagine I'm following the fresh tracks of Professor Almon Thompson. He was a geographer with Major John Wesley Powell's survey party, which mapped this last, unexplored region of the West in 1872. Professor Thompson named Pleasant Creek, noting that it was "a clear stream flowing through groves of Cottonwood, and entitled to the name we gave it."

Thompson first saw the stream at its source high on Boulder Mountain, which he called the Aquarius Plateau for the many lakes that dot its rolling surface. Rising to 11,000 feet about ten miles upstream from my path, this forty-mile-long plateau presides over Capitol Reef on the west. It is one of several high plateaus in southern Utah that mark the junction of two great geologic provinces: the Basin and Range and the Colorado Plateau.

From the brink of Boulder Mountain—near Pleasant Creek's headwaters—the view eastward toward the Waterpocket Fold and the blue peaks of the Henry Mountains inspires poetry. The forested, lava-rimmed plateau drops off into a wonderland of canyons, castles, temples, towers, thrones, domes, and knobs, all shaded in buff, gray, and vermilion. Almon Thompson, however, was faced with finding a route through this territory, and not surprisingly, he described a landscape more imposing than poetic: "It is cut by deep cañons and looks impassable."

The survey party's difficult descent from Boulder Mountain was chronicled by Frederick Dellenbaugh, Thompson's young assistant. According to Dellenbaugh's diaries, they encountered a small encampment of Ute Indians, whose chief signed accurate directions to the Unknown Mountains, later named the Henrys. The following morning the explorers worked their way down-canyon, their progress frequently slowed by false turns and precipitous cliffs. As darkness fell, they encamped near a small waterpocket that provided a "full drink" for the thirsty men and their animals. The next day, to get the horses over a steep rock shelf to additional water, two men had to put their "shoulders to the haunches of some of the horses to 'boost' them, while other men pulled on a strong halter from above." Soon after this event, the group reached lower Pleasant Creek, and from that point forward they had easy going to the Henrys.

No such travails trouble my saunter along Pleasant Creek. I linger lazily under the cool shade of a cottonwood, gazing up at walls of Wingate Sandstone that whirl into a blue, blue sky. Above me, the cliff faces bear a patina of bronze varnish and are sculpted into

*S*everal species of Indian paintbrush are found in Capitol Reef. This wildflower grows in most of the Park's habitats, and, depending on elevation, its showy blooms are seen from March to October. © ROD PLANCK.

glorious curves and alcoves. Rabbitbrush and olive-green junipers dot the higher terraces. Indian paintbrush dash the desert with crimson; I pause to probe the showy red bracts of a paintbrush to find the true yellow flower hidden within. Pale lavender thistles and poison milkweed bloom beside the creek. Violet-green swallows dart overhead. A coyote track is impressed in the damp mud. Tresses of green algae sway in the creek, and water striders furiously skate across the backeddies.

Pleasant Creek swings to and fro as it presses on a few more miles through the Fold. I cross the stream numerous times, soon giving up on the idea of dry boots. As I assume the rhythm of the creek, I'm reminded that nature is in charge here. I start to let go of my daily trappings and concerns and open other senses to nature's wonders.

These days, to be "in nature" requires a conscious effort to extricate ourselves from the comfortable, controlled environment in which we live. Nature has become a place we go to, rather than something that we are part of. The Latin root word for nature is *nasci*, which means "to be born." I too have become one of those who seek out such places. For me, Pleasant Creek is a place of rebirth.

Splashing on, I come upon a place where the stream swirls into a stairstep series of potholes carved into smooth pink bedrock. Their lure is irresistible. I cool off in the pools and dry on the warm rocks, realizing this enchanting spot is the surprise Pleasant Creek had waiting for me.

*H*ikers who venture through the sinuous gorge of Sulphur Creek will encounter this lovely grotto. Sulphur Creek is one of the few places in Capitol Reef where White Rim Sandstone is exposed; this is the oldest formation in the Park, dating back more than 230 million years.

© SCOTT T. SMITH.

*B*uilt into a cliff that overlooks the lower Fremont River, this structure
exhibits the masonry work that became one of the defining characteristics of
the prehistoric Fremont people. © JEFF GNASS. *The most visible cultural legacy
of the Fremont, however, is their distinctive rock art. Fremont petroglyphs
and pictographs are among the Park's most intriguing and vulnerable
treasures. Opposite page, clockwise from upper left:* © STEPHEN TRIMBLE.
© DAVID EDE. © GEORGE H. H. HUEY. © LYNN RADEKA.

*F*ruita receives an average of seven inches of precipitation each year, and about half of it comes in the form of snow. It is a special treat to visit the Park after a fresh dusting of snow. © TOM TILL.

Opposite: The Fremont River has carved a rugged gorge on the western edge of the Park where it makes a steep, 1,000-foot descent from Torrey to Fruita. © SCOTT T. SMITH.

Capitol Reef is endowed with many miles of hiking trails, such as the route that leads to this spectacular perch above the Castle. © DAVID PLATT. *Opposite: Beginning in the 1880s, stockmen began to cross the Waterpocket Fold at a break in its thick layer of Navajo Sandstone. This historic route is now a graded dirt road known as the Burr Trail. It switchbacks over the Fold, ascending 800 feet in half a mile and providing a rare cross-section view of the monocline.* © SCOTT T. SMITH.

*D*ozens of scenic slot canyons drain the Waterpocket Fold, and many of them contain subsurface water that sustains small groves of boxelder. © GEORGE H. H. HUEY.

Opposite: Only a handful of perennial creeks flow through the Waterpocket Fold, including Pleasant Creek, which was once home to prehistoric people and, later, to early pioneers. © D. A. HORCHNER.

VALLEY OF CATHEDRALS

Heading for territory I've never visited, I inch my truck through turbid, foot-deep water to ford the Fremont River. My aim is the farthest northern reaches of Capitol Reef: South Desert and Cathedral Valley.

I travel a dirt road into North Blue Flats, following a parched streambed appropriately called Dry Wash. The landscape soon makes a dramatic transition; rocky desert scrub gives way to badlands, where soft clays and shales of the Morrison Formation are exposed in the Bentonite Hills.

The clay mineral that gives the Bentonite Hills their name has a remarkable ability to swell, increasing six or seven times in volume when wet. After a rain, the clay turns into an impossibly slippery goo, locally known as gumbo. For those on foot or in a vehicle, the badlands gumbo makes tricky going. When the clay dries, it shrinks again. The endless cycle of swelling and shrinking gives the land a wrinkled texture that resembles elephant skin.

The oranges, rusts, mauves, and grays of these rolling hills melt together like tie-dyed velvet, inviting me to take a closer look on foot. Rounded black boulders repose on the hills, like bowling balls

It is a country of long views, a spacious country, yet the horizon, however distant, is always clearly defined, the ridgelines providing a proper edge to the immensity of the sky.
—**Edward Geary**
The Proper Edge of the Sky,
1992

The multi-hued sediments of the Bentonite Hills were laid down in an inland lake about 140 million years ago (above). © JOHN TELFORD. *A shaft of sunlight illuminates a solitary monolith in the South Desert (above, right).* © WM. B. DEWEY. *Preceding pages: The Temples of the Sun and Moon soar above Lower Cathedral Valley (left).* © TOM TILL. *The wide-open spaces of Upper Cathedral Valley occupy the northern edge of the Park (right).* © JEFF NICHOLAS.

placed with great care by the hands of a giant. Tiny stones and pebbles perch on individual pedestals of clay, helping armor the soft sediments against erosion. I think of bones, perhaps because the Morrison Formation is well known for containing fossils of dinosaurs. But what I think might be bones are only more rocks that look like bones.

Low, gray-green bushes dot the hills' rubbled surface. These hardy shrubs are shadscale, one of the few things able to bully through the tough crust and survive the Morrison's salty, selenium-rich soil. Scattered amid the gullies and washes that snake through the hills are dried stems of desert trumpet. This member of the buckwheat family derives its common name—and its species name *inflatum*—from its inflated stems, which swell after tiny wasps deposit their eggs inside them.

I return to my truck, leaving behind the austere beauty of the badlands. The road proceeds for many miles and gently climbs into a woodland of pinyon and juniper. After parking at Upper South Desert Overlook, I creep up to the edge of a 500-foot cliff and peer over the precipice. A grand sweep of wild, lonely country stretches before me. A brisk wind is blowing, and I slip on a warm shirt. High above, a hawk circles dreamily. Over my shoulder, feeling close enough to touch, are the black-green heights of Thousand Lake Mountain. Aspen in their autumn glory spangle the bulky shoulders of the mountain, like epaulets on a soldier's coat.

Such a commanding view of the countryside is special. More often, my explorations in Capitol Reef lead to canyons, where I'm flanked by soaring walls of stone and alert for flash floods. But here the setting is wide open; a dome of blue sky arcs over a seemingly infinite wilderness. Particularly momentous is the vista of the Waterpocket Fold, swelling out of the side of Thousand Lake Mountain like the headwaters of a great, holy river.

Solitary monoliths of Entrada Sandstone jut skyward from the floor of upper Cathedral Valley below me. Those who named the valley must have thought the monoliths looked like cathedrals; to me, they resemble stone-faced totem poles. They appear immutable, but fan-shaped piles of sand at their bases, the same buff-pink color as the formations themselves, are evidence that erosion is at work

Runoff from melting glaciers deposited these basaltic boulders (foreground) and also carried away much of the soft Entrada Sandstone in the basin below, leaving a 450-foot-high monolith known as Temple Rock. © LARRY VENSEL.

here too. As the sun eases lower in the sky, the light richens and the tall monoliths cast long shadows across the flats.

Around me, soft fragrant sagebrush and bounteous buffaloberry grow beneath dwarf junipers and pinyon pines. The sights, sounds, and smells of this diminutive forest are the essence of the upland Southwest. The stubby brown pinyon cones have opened, but they contain no seeds. Poking in the dry duff beneath the trees, all I find are last year's faded, empty hulls. From nearby treetops come the haunting cries of pinyon jays. The noisy flock probably harvested the cones I inspected.

I marvel at the knowledge these birds have of this woodland. In late summer, the jays collect and bury pinyon seeds in thousands of communal caches strategically located near breeding areas. The birds return to feed from their caches throughout the year. During the jays' breeding season, from February through April, the seeds are an especially important food source. The jays don't retrieve all the seeds, however, and one day a seed will give birth to a new pinyon. It's a beautifully beneficial arrangement: tree sustains bird and bird sustains tree.

It is hard to imagine, but the pinyons, junipers, and desert shrubs that surround me have not always been here. Our knowledge of how plant life has changed in the Southwest is due in large part to the habits of a small, shy rodent: the packrat. These animals construct their nests from every conceivable material: plant stems, leaves, seeds, bones, and even the dung of other animals. Generation after generation, packrats occupy the same nest, sometimes using the structure for thousands of years. Over time, the nest becomes saturated with packrat urine, which preserves the accumulated plant matter. Thus, the packrats' middens serve as nature's unique time capsules.

Paleoecologists, scientists who study past environments, search out packrat middens, take samples from them, and identify the contents. Some middens from Capitol Reef date back more than 10,000 years and mostly contain Douglas-fir needles. Today, there are no Douglas-fir growing around me; they are found only at higher, more moist elevations. From my perch at the overlook, the view would have been strikingly different 11,000 years ago, during the last ice age. The air would have been much colder, as glaciers breathed down from Thousand Lake Mountain, and the land would have been forested with tall conifers.

Between 11,000 and 8,000 years ago, the glaciers receded and the climate throughout much of the continent generally grew warmer and drier. A big shift came about 8,000 years ago, and all of the Southwest, including Capitol Reef, became increasingly arid. Plants that are now abundant, such as Mormon tea, rabbitbrush, and pinyon pine, gradually became dominant because they were able to adapt to the hot summers and cold winters that now define Capitol Reef's high desert climate.

The landscape of South Desert and Cathedral Valley looks eternal. I think what I see today is what was always here. But change is nature's universal theme. The middens of the little packrats tell us so.

*T*hese fast-eroding spires in Upper Cathedral Valley are remnants of a once-continuous, 600-foot-deep layer of Entrada Sandstone (above). © JEFF NICHOLAS.
Shrubs such as Mormon tea (left) and serviceberry (right) are well adapted to the arid climate of the South Desert (opposite, above). © FRED HIRSCHMANN.
The longnose leopard lizard is one of twenty-four species of reptiles that are found in the Park (opposite, below). © ROD PLANCK.

About a hundred species of common wildflowers are found in Capitol Reef. Colorado four o'clock grows in shady areas of the pinyon-juniper woodland.
© FRED HIRSCHMANN.

Opposite page, clockwise from upper left: A natural bouquet brightens the slickrock. © GARY MOON.
In certain years, wildflowers carpet the desert. © LARRY VENSEL.
Golden sego lily occurs only on the Colorado Plateau. © ROD PLANCK.
The deep red bloom of claret cup cactus is a favorite of Park visitors.
© FRED HIRSCHMANN.

*T*he Fremont River was the source of irrigation water that made farming possible here. The river also occasionally rampaged during summer thunderstorms, and three small agricultural communities downriver from Fruita were abandoned following devastating floods. © LARRY ULRICH.

Opposite: The families of Fruita depended primarily on fruit sales for their yearly income, but they also raised other crops, such as vegetables, alfalfa, and sorghum.
© TOM TILL.

Like many arches in Capitol Reef, aptly named Saddle Arch is only accessible by hiking. Eroded in Kayenta Sandstone, Saddle Arch is found near the crest of the Waterpocket Fold in Upper Muley Twist Canyon. © FRED HIRSCHMANN.

These striated columns are composed of Moenkopi mudstones, siltstones, and sandstones; the rocks' different hues and textures reflect the changing conditions as sediments were deposited in a shallow sea to form the Moenkopi Formation about 200 to 230 million years ago. © SCOTT T. SMITH.

Near Fruita, young, water-loving cottonwoods flutter in the breeze, their spring foliage framed against ancient, burnished cliffs that began as desert dunes. © WILLIAM NEILL. Opposite: The Bentonite Hills are dotted with volcanic boulders that were carried in by glacial runoff; these badlands represent yet another chapter in Capitol Reef's incredible geologic story. © JEFF NICHOLAS.

OCTOBER JOURNEY

Near an old oil drillers' site on Big Thompson Mesa, a faint path drops into Halls Creek. Cairns mark the route, the only break in the cliffs for miles in either direction. I look over the edge and gulp hard. I've been this way before.

Starting down, my knees balk at what they're asked to do. I clutch the branches of shrubs for support, bolstered by words of encouragement from my husband, Michael. Our descent goes well, and we soon enter the wide valley of Halls Creek.

We pause under a lone cottonwood dressed in October gold. From here, Halls Creek heads due south, flanked by the soaring swell of the Waterpocket Fold to the west and by the impenetrable cliffs of Halls Mesa to the east. This country is the remotest of the remote in Capitol Reef.

We could follow the meandering, moist creekbed, stepping from boulder to boulder, or take a shortcut across the flats along an old wagon road. We choose the shortcut, a sandy trail first broken by horse hooves, boot heels, and wooden wheels. The path is fringed by sagebrush, Indian ricegrass, and prickly pear adorned with ripe red fruit. One of the cactus fruits lies near the entrance to a burrow

Hold your hands out over the earth as over a flame . . . rest your spirit in her solitary places. For the gifts of life are the earth's and they are given to all.

—Henry Beston
The Outermost House,
1949

In 1882 a small party of Mormon pioneers traveled down Halls Creek in wagons similar to this one (above). © DAVID PLATT.
Charles Hall's trail from Escalante to the Colorado River followed the rugged drainage of Muley Twist Canyon (above, right). © GARY MOON.
Shady pools reflect the vertical cliffs of Halls Creek Narrows (opposite). © DAVID EDE.
Preceding pages: The striking uplift of the Waterpocket Fold greets explorers to the Halls Creek area (left). © WILLIAM M. SMITHEY, JR.
Hikers encounter a vast slickrock wilderness in and around Halls Creek (right). © DAVID EDE.

where ants carry away its seeds.

After a couple of miles, I shed my pack and seek the irresistible shade of another cottonwood. The only sound is the rattling of the burnished leaves in the breeze. A woodpecker flies to a branch in the tree. From a nearby hillock, Michael calls me over to see the translucent molted skin of a snake twined through a rabbitbrush.

As we walk the old road, I think about the journey of Mormon pioneers through Halls Creek, also in October, but in 1882. Leading the way was Charles Hall, for whom this creek is named. A native of Maine, a carpenter, bricklayer, and boatbuilder, Hall came to Utah in 1850. In the winter of 1879-1880, he was part of the epic Hole-in-the-Rock Expedition, in which a group of Latter-day Saints lowered wagons and stock two thousand feet down a precipitous break in a cliff to reach the Colorado River. Hall and his sons ferried the Saints across the river, and the pioneers continued on to the San Juan River, where they settled the town of Bluff.

Soon after this episode, Charles Hall began his search for a more accessible route to the Colorado River. He blazed a trail east from Escalante, over the Waterpocket Fold, and south down Halls Creek to its junction with the river. Here, he built a wooden ferry, ten feet by thirty feet, and went into business. He charged his customers five dollars a wagon and seventy-five cents a horse to carry them across the Colorado's swift current.

In late October 1882, a small wagon train of Saints set out to join the settlers at Bluff. They followed Hall's new "road" through Harris Wash, up Silver Falls Creek and across the Circle Cliffs, through Muley Twist Canyon, then down Halls Creek to Halls Crossing. Among them was Josephine Wood, known to all as "Aunt Jody." Her diary entries vividly recount their travails. "Started . . . with great sorrow and weeping because of parting from all of our dear friends and relatives . . . we had nothing to do but to lie back in our wagons and think of those we had left behind." As they moved overland to the Waterpocket Fold, blowing wind, scarce water, and rough country became the order of each grueling day. The women and children often had to push the wagons through knee-deep sand. At one point Aunt Jody declared: "It is the most God-forsaken and wild looking country that was ever traveled." Their salvation was the waterpockets, which still held rainwater from late-summer cloudbursts.

The Saints finally arrived at Halls Crossing on November 3, where they had to face one more ordeal. "Now it is our turn—O pray for us!" beseeched Aunt Jody. She and her children got inside their wagon, which was then driven onto the raft and lashed down. "The

A thunderstorm unleashes its fury over the Fold at dusk. Hikers in slot canyons, such as Halls Narrows, are advised to be aware of the potential for flash floods associated with storms. © SCOTT T. SMITH.

men started rowing, and down the raft and all went into the water with a splash. My heart went faint, I went blind and clung to my babies. I shall never forget my feeling as we went down into the water, and my fear of the wagon going off into the swift-flowing river." But they survived the crossing, and once they were safe on the opposite bank Aunt Jody and her companions "did thank our Heavenly Father."

Our trek down Halls Creek is not nearly so eventful. We sidestep slow-moving pools of water and try to avoid the slippery gray mud left by a recent flood. The water and mud are reminders of the paradox of this place: having too much water or scarcely enough.

One summer afternoon, while on another trip into the canyons of Halls Creek, dark clouds gathered over the Fold and we decided to pack up and make a hasty departure. When we were halfway up the trail, the storm swept in.

We took refuge under a huge overhanging boulder. Lightning snapped in the void before us and waterfalls poured over the Fold. As we stared wide-eyed, Halls Creek started to flow. Everything I'd read about desert flash floods had not prepared me for the sight of the proverbial wall of water pouring downstream like molten copper, bank to bank, blocking access and carelessly plucking up anything in its path.

From the supposed safety of our boulder shelter, we watched this drama for a long time, happy to be high and dry above Halls Creek. Then, the trail in front of us turned into a stream of water.

Michael suggested that if the rock we were sitting under showed any sign of movement, we should hightail it out, storm or no storm. The thought had not even crossed my mind, but I heeded the warning. A geologist by training, he knew rocks can move. The boulder never budged, and when the storm ceased we trudged out to the mesa top.

I recall this adventure as we approach Halls Narrows, our destination for the night. The Narrows is a three-mile stretch of tight twists and turns, a delectable detour before Halls Creek resumes its final, no-nonsense course southward to Halls Crossing, now submerged beneath Lake Powell.

Just when our bodies begin to weary from the day's journey, the Narrows come into view. We unpack our gear beneath a great vaulted alcove of Navajo Sandstone, a chamber that could easily seat a symphony orchestra. The walls arc 180 degrees above us. The creek, rippling softly in the background, is lined with water-loving willows, oaks, boxelders, barberries, and cottonwoods. A hanging garden of brilliant emerald maidenhair ferns drapes a sandstone cleft.

As we start supper, the sharp crack of falling rock leads us to examine the boulders on the sand around us. We look up. It's all too clear where they've come from. Just as we're trying to decide whether we've chosen the best spot, a small chunk of rock clunks onto our sleeping pads. Deliberations cease. We pick up everything and move a short distance back upstream to an open, sandy site.

Bats flutter by in the twilight. The first stars shimmer in the lens of sky overhead. As dark flows in, the cloud of the Milky Way follows the curve of the rock above us. Delphinus, the Dolphin, leaps

Halls Creek Narrows is a place of beauty and solitude. At the Narrows, the creek has incised a deep, meandering gorge through the Navajo Sandstone. © STEPHEN TRIMBLE.

through the sky: summer stars changing places with winter stars. The moon rises, just past full, and washes the walls with silver. It is a still, still night, filled with dreams.

Near dawn, a canyon wren sings us awake, and a sliver of morning sunlight slides down the alcove wall. We watch to see whether the light will reach the canyon bottom. It doesn't. After a cup of coffee, I wrest myself from the cocoon of my sleeping bag, looking forward to a day dawdling through the Narrows, going as far as we wish, without backpacks. Ravens fly over. One squawks just to hear itself squawk, or perhaps to urge me to get going so it can investigate my pack.

We filter water, fill bottles, stuff a day pack with lunch, and start walking. Our progress is slow because there's so much to examine: the velvety yellow leaves of the boxelders, their twinned key fruits hanging in pendulous chains; a strange brown mushroom sprouting in the wet sand; stiff scouring rush flattened by the last pulse of floodwater; a hefty chunk of petrified wood brought downstream from some distant point; a tiny canyon tree frog.

Slippery mud waits to suck us in as we step carefully across it. In pools where I can't see bottom, I wade in and sink down another foot, slip, and go in up to my waist. To dry out, I perch on a sunny boulder and pour the thick silt from my boots. I spot a small alcove hidden by a thicket of Gambel oak and go up to investigate. Poised on the alcove's sandy floor is the skull of a bighorn ram.

With each new bend of the creek, the view is more stunning. I round a corner and gaze downstream at a glowing, backlit

Although Capitol Reef has an arid climate, amphibians such as this leopard frog are found near Halls Creek and in other moist drainages of the Park (above).

© STEPHEN TRIMBLE.

Cottonwood is the largest deciduous tree in Capitol Reef. It grows at lower elevations of the Park wherever there is plentiful surface or subsurface moisture (opposite).

© WILLIAM M. SMITHEY, JR.

cottonwood that stands in perfect composition. It's an image forever preserved in my memory, like a wildflower pressed between the pages of a book. Perhaps that sight brings on a late-afternoon melancholy. As I sit by the stream sipping cool water from my metal cup, I sense the hope and promise of morning sliding away, replaced with an urge to go back, settle in for the night, cook dinner, stay warm. I know this feeling. It's a conflict between utter happiness and contentment in this wild, unpeopled place and my human desire for a secure nest.

We wind back through the Narrows, making camp on a generous, flat spit of sand. High, thin clouds float over the Fold, but evaporate in the dusk. We see more stars and more sky than we did the night before. There are more constellations to name, more stories to tell. It's a long night with a bright moon that never sets. At dawn, pink mare's tails fringe the top of Halls Mesa. A jubilant morning chorus of coyotes spills out of the hills. Frost decorates the sleeping bags. We linger in camp, cleaning up, washing breakfast dishes, packing away damp, dirty clothes. We start back in the coolness, passing now-familiar landmarks.

We came to Halls Creek to watch and to listen. We have seen no one during our three days here. We didn't expect to. How different it must have been for Josephine Wood and the other settlers of this country, who came not to recreate, but to try to wrest a living from this hard country. Like us, were they sometimes overwhelmed by the beauty and the silence of this magnificent landscape? Did they find solace? I don't know, but I hope so.

Water is surprisingly abundant in Capitol Reef's arid, high-desert climate. Sulphur Creek is one of several year-round streams that flow through the park.
© SCOTT T. SMITH.

Opposite page, clockwise from upper left: The Fremont River thunders across bedrock. © ROD PLANCK.
A gentle cascade polishes the slickrock. © GARY MOON.
A deep waterpocket is worn into Navajo Sandstone. © D. A. HORCHNER.
Quiet water reflects a colorful canyon. © GARY MOON.

*T*he first rays of daylight shine upon
the Temple of the Sun and highlight
patterns of erosion on nearby
sandstone outcrops. © CARR CLIFTON.
*Opposite: A lone pinyon pine grows
from a notch in the cliff high above
Grand Wash.* © GEORGE H. H. HUEY.

*C*apitol Reef encompasses a vast and incomparable landscape. The Park preserves breathtaking scenery, large wilderness areas, and a fascinating pioneer community. It is one of the treasures of the American West.